2465

1/86

2.99

J
599.01
Sattler, Helen Roney
Noses are Special

2465

NOSES
ARE SPECIAL

Helen Roney Sattler

illustrated by
Charles Cox

ABINGDON • Nashville

Noses Are Special

Copyright © 1982 by Abingdon
All Rights Reserved

Library of Congress Cataloging in Publication Data

Sattler, Helen Roney.
  Noses are special.
    Summary: Discusses what a nose can do and why
some animals have specially adapted noses.
    1. Nose—Juvenile literature. [1. Nose] I. Title.
QL947.S27   599.01'826   81-20648   AACR2
ISBN 0-687-28120-2

To my granddaughter,
Branda Lea Gatz

Noses are special things.
They come in all shapes and sizes.
Some are big.
Some are little.
Some are long and ropey.
Some are short and stubby.
Others are hooked or turned up.

But what are noses good for?
One of the things a nose is good for is smelling.
Noses help animals find their dinners.
Sometimes noses help animals find their mates.
Other times noses warn of danger.
Many animals depend upon their nose
    to tell them if an enemy is near.
Smelling is the most important thing a nose does.

But noses are also for breathing—
    warm spring breezes, hot summer air, or cold wintry blasts.
Noses can warm the cold air
    and moisten the hot dry air.
Noses also strain out the dust.

Almost any nose can smell or breathe,
   but some noses can do other things as well.
That is why they come in all shapes and sizes.

Sometimes people don't like the kind of nose they have.
But what if animals wanted different kinds of noses?

What would happen if the hippopotamus wanted a nose like an elephant's?
A hippo's nose is just right for a hippopotamus.
These animals can stand all day in the water
   with just the tip of their nose sticking out.
Their nose brings lots of air into their lungs,
   and they can stay under water a long time
   without having to come up to breathe.

An elephant with a nose like a rhinoceros' wouldn't be an elephant.
Without their long trunk-nose elephants couldn't eat or drink.
Elephants use their trunk like arms and hands.
They can pick up tiny bits of food, a blade of grass,
   or a peanut and put them into their mouth.
Sometimes elephants use their nose to give themselves shower baths.
They hold their trunk straight up and blow water out over their back.
When they are angry or want to warn another elephant of danger,
   they can use their trunk as a trumpet.
It is a good thing for elephants
that their nose is not like the rhinoceros'.

Wouldn't a rhinoceros look silly with a nose like an anteater's?
The horns on a rhinoceros' nose are fierce weapons.
Sometimes these horns grow longer than you are tall.
Rhinoceroses' large nostrils give them a keen sense of smell.
This is important because they have very poor eyesight.
When they keep their nose pointed into the wind,
   it warns them of danger.

What if anteaters wanted a nose like the camel's?
Anteaters use their long tubular nose to catch their dinner.
Anteaters can't see or hear well,
    so they hold their nose close to the ground as they walk
    and smell out ants.
The anteater's nozzle-shaped nose
    is just right for poking into anthills.
It has no nostrils to get full of sand and dirt.
At the end of the snout there is just one small hole
    through which anteaters breathe, smell,
        and poke out their long sticky tongue.
Anteaters would get very hungry if they had the nose of a camel.

If a camel had a nose like a pig's, it would get full of sand.
The camel's long, narrow nose is just right for living on a desert.
It has slits for nostrils, which can be closed to keep out sand.
A heavy fringe of hair around the nostrils strains out dust
    and helps protect them from flying sand.
A camel's nose also has big chambers to moisten
    the hot dry air that would otherwise hurt their lungs.
A pig's flat nose wouldn't suit the camel at all.

If pigs had a nose like the moose's, they couldn't root in the mud.
Pigs use their long agile snout to sniff out
   roots, bulbs, and tubers they like to eat.
The flat part is very sensitive, something like a giant finger.
Pigs need it to dig up food buried underground.
It is a very good nose for pigs.

Moose would have problems if they had a nose like a dog's.
They need their large bulbous nose.
The big nostrils act as a warming chamber to warm the cold wintry air.
They also bring in lots of air
    so moose can stay under water a long time
    to eat the water lilies and duck-weed
    that grow on the bottoms of lakes and ponds.
It is the best kind of nose for a moose.

What if dogs had a nose like the star-nosed mole's?
How could they bury bones and track animals?
A dog's conical nose is just right for poking into holes and under rocks.
It is the best smeller in the whole world,
  but it makes a good burying tool, too.
After dogs drop their bones into a hole,
  they use their nose to push the dirt over it.
Then they tamp the dirt down firmly with the tip.
The nostrils are comma-shaped and can be closed to keep out dirt.
It's a perfect nose for a dog.

What would it be like for moles to have a nose like the bat's?
They couldn't burrow under the ground.
Moles use their nose as a wedge or ram
   to push and shovel soil aside as they build their long tunnels.
Because they can't see, they also need their sensitive nose
   to feel their way toward insects and earthworms.
The ring of fleshy fingers
   circling the nose-tip of the star-nosed mole is super-sensitive.
These fingers tell them everything they need to know
   about their underground world.
The mole's nose is good for burrowing; a bat's nose is better for flying.

Bats couldn't get around if they had a nose like a coati-mundi's.
Bats fly at night and can't see very well,
   but because of their very special nose they can fly
   through a woods without hitting a tree.
Bats have a very good sense of smell,
   but they use their nose in another special way.
They use it like a sonar
   to send out supersonic sounds through their nostrils.
The sound strikes an object and bounces back to the bats' ears,
   warning them of an obstacle in their path.
No other nose can do that.

Imagine the coati-mundi with a nose like an alligator's.
Coatis are very curious animals
  who like to investigate everything.
They need a long pointed nose
  to poke into every hole or crevice.
The coati's nose is flexible and can bend around corners and trees.
But their nose is tough, too.
They sometimes use it as a tool
  to dig up worms and insects.
With an alligator-type nose they couldn't do that at all.

And what would alligators do with the nose that an elephant seal has?
An alligator's nose is just right for catching food in shallow water.
Their nostrils are on top at the tip of their long, broad snout,
  and they can float all day with just the tip of it sticking out.
Their nose will tell them when a tasty meal comes along.
Why should they want any other kind?

How would elephant seals look with a short flat nose like a duck's?
Their long floppy nose makes elephant seals special.
Most of the time these noses hang limply below their mouth.
But when elephant seals are angry
   or want to frighten an enemy,
   they blow their nose up until it looks like the bulb
   of an enormous bullhorn, and then they honk!
And if the seals are frightened or want to dive for food,
   they can fill their nose with enough air
   to stay under water for eight minutes.

If ducks had a nose like a crab's, they wouldn't have a nose at all.
They couldn't stand on their head to catch fish at the bottom of the pond.
Ducks use their beak like shovels
   to probe the mud for crayfish and worms.
Ducks couldn't get along without their broad flat nose.

There are all kinds of noses in the world.
Most of them are for breathing or smelling.
But there are some like hands, shovels, nozzels, or trumpets.
Some are even sonars.
But every nose is shaped just right
    and is just the right size
    to take care of the special needs
    of the animal who wears it.